·TESCO· ·COOKERY· ·COLLECTION·

COOKING
FOR KIDS

TESCO

Published exclusively for Tesco Stores Ltd.
Delamare Road, Cheshunt, Herts, EN8 9SL
by Cathay Books, 59 Grosvenor Street, London W1

First published 1985

© Cathay Books 1985

ISBN 0 86178 307 7

Printed in Hong Kong

ACKNOWLEDGEMENTS

The publishers would like to thank the following companies
for their kindness in providing materials and equipment
used in the photography for this book
Hamley's Toy Shop, Regent Street, London W1
The Cocktail Shop, Neal Street, London WC2
The General Store, Longacre, London WC2
Way In, Harrods, Knightsbridge, London SW1
Wedgewood Showrooms, Wigmore Street, London W1
Young World, Kensington High Street, London W8

We would also like to thank the following who
were concerned in the preparation of the book.

Series Art Director Pedro Pra-Lopez
Editor Barbara Croxford
Photographer Alan Duns (page 54-5 James Jackson)
Stylist Paula Lovell
Food prepared for photography by Caroline Ellwood

CONTENTS

NOTE

Standard spoon measurements are used in all recipes

1 tablespoon (tbls) = one 15 ml spoon
1 teaspoon (tsp) = one 5 ml spoon
All spoon measures are level

All eggs are sizes 3 or 4 (standard) unless otherwise stated.

For all recipes, quantities are given in both
metric and imperial measures. Follow either set
but not a mixture of both, as they are not interchangeable.

W̲e set up our Consumer Advisory Service in response to the many pleas for information and cooking ideas we received from our customers. It is run by our team of qualified home economists who answer queries, offer practical advice on cookery and the home and give talks and demonstrations on new products and equipment.

The resounding success of the service and the continued demand for more and more recipes and information has now prompted us to produce our own special range of Tesco Cookery Books.

Our series starts with 12 books, each one focusing on an area that our customers have shown particular interest in. Each book contains practical background information on the chosen subject and concentrates on a wide selection of carefully tested recipes, each one illustrated in colour.

Cooking For Kids is full of bright new ideas to help you break away from the monotony of baked beans and bangers-and-mash – without adding hours to your preparation time. All the recipes have been styled especially for kids, using many of their favourite ingredients in amusing, eye-catching presentations. At the same time the principles of good, sensible nutrition have been followed throughout, to promote the healthy growth that every child should enjoy.

I very much hope you and your children will enjoy looking through the pages which follow, trying out the recipes and above all tasting and enjoying the results. Happy Cooking!

Carey Dennis, senior home economist, Tesco Stores Ltd.

INTRODUCTION

Children's meals need to be nutritionally balanced and temptingly presented to encourage them to eat well.

Pre-school age children grow particularly fast and therefore need plenty of the right foods to give them the vital protein and energy they require: lean meat, fish, eggs, cheese, bread, beans, cereals and milk all supply these. It is very important that they should have milk every day as it provides calcium which is essential for growth of bones and teeth, as well as other minerals and vitamins: if your child does not like the taste of milk to drink, try making interestingly flavoured milk shakes and include plenty in sauces and puddings.

Pre-school children often have small appetites, so offer them small, attractively served quantities of food rather than a daunting plateful – they can always come back for seconds. Young children's appetites also vary constantly – lots of activity in the fresh air makes them hungry, but on a rainy day spent indoors they may not want much to eat at all. Never force a child to eat more than it wants.

School children and teenagers need plenty of calcium, phosphorus and vitamins D and C which work together to make sturdy bones, teeth and gums. Calcium is obtained from cheese, yoghurt and green vegetables as well as milk. Phosphorus is found with calcium in milk and dairy foods as well as in meat, fish and a wide range of other foods. Vitamin D is present in oily fish, eggs, margarine, butter and cheese, but, more importantly, we also make our own supply when the skin is exposed to sunshine, so encourage your children to play outside when the weather is fine. Vitamin C is found in fresh fruit and vegetables.

Make sure your child gets the best start diet-wise by cutting down on sweet, sugary foods: most children have a naturally sweet tooth, but if this is over-indulged, there is a real possibility that they will grow into obese adults with teeth problems. Ration sweets by keeping a supply in a tin and allowing one or two a day – ideally after lunch. Encourage children from the earliest possible age to develop a taste for *natural* sweet foods such as fresh fruit, raisins, dates and honey.

Unfortunately, many of the other snack foods children love also have disadvantages – they are high in fat (and sometimes salt as well), two things we're being encouraged to eat less of. These foods include crisps and salted or 'dry-roasted' peanuts.

The important thing is to keep a sense of balance – a bag of crisps occasionally won't do much harm but 3 or 4 a day will be bad for a child. Try and balance your children's meals – so if you give them a fatty food like sausages or pastry, don't give them chips or crisps with it. Accompany it with a salad or fresh vegetables.

The recipes in this book have been arranged to provide a wide range of ideas to suit children's varying eating patterns. Numbers of servings have been given for each recipe, but this may vary depending on age and appetites.

When school children return home, they are often starving! Between-meal snacks shouldn't really be necessary but at times like these offer them a piece of fruit, cube of cheese, a raw carrot to munch, or a handful of nuts and raisins. Children will benefit from a substantial high tea or supper rather than filling up on cakes and biscuits directly after school, and all children love having their friends round to play and stay for a snack or tea. There is a varied selection of tempting dishes for such occasions.

Children often need a packed lunch, to replace school dinner, or to take on a picnic or other outing. This is going to be one of their main meals so it needs to be nutritious and imaginative. Sandwiches and rolls are always very popular: wholemeal bread is much more nourishing than white, but some children do not like brown bread, so meet them half way and make sandwiches with one slice of white bread and one of wholemeal. Pies and pastries are ideal too as the main part of the lunch, and an accompanying salad can easily be packed in a polythene container. Some children may not enjoy a straightforward lettuce-based salad, so try adding vegetable crudités — strips of carrot, cucumber or red or green pepper — to the lunch box, with a small container of savoury dip. Provide a piece of fresh fruit and don't forget to pack a drink.

Most children do love cakes and biscuits, and this section of the book gives many delicious ideas. If you bake your own, you can be sure that they are made with fresh, natural ingredients, as well as cutting down on the cost. But remember, these foods do tend to be high in sugar and fat — don't let your child over indulge in these instead of other, healthier foods. Store cakes and biscuits in airtight containers as soon as they are baked and cooled completely — they stay in peak condition that way.

The last section in the book is on party food — the highlight of every child's birthday party. There are a few points to remember when planning a successful children's party. Think carefully about where to hold it: if hiring a hall, book well in advance. How many guests will there be? If you ask more than eight, you may need the help of another adult. Under-fives may often have Mum in tow too, which expands the numbers considerably. Allocate yourself a budget for food, prizes and small take-home gifts.

Children's party food should be colourful and fun, combining imaginative ideas alongside familiar favourites. Provide roughly equal amounts of savoury and sweet items. Choose some of the following: tiny sandwiches cut into exciting shapes; small pieces of quiche or pizza; cocktail sausages on sticks or sausage rolls — dips, crisps and other savoury nibbles; biscuits, cakes, ice cream and individual jellies or trifles. Provide squash and fizzy drinks, preferably the sugar-free type; older children might appreciate a Caribbean cocktail.

Funny face salad

SERVES 4

1 small iceberg lettuce, shredded
2 hard-boiled eggs, shelled and
*   quartered*
2 large tomatoes, quartered
100 g (4 oz) Edam cheese, cut into 4
*   equal wedges*
4 tbls thousand island dressing
mustard and cress, to garnish

Arrange lettuce in 4 individual salad bowls. Arrange the eggs as ears, tomatoes as eyebrows and cheese as a mouth on top of the lettuce to make a face.

Spoon the thousand island dressing evenly over the lettuce to make eyes and use the mustard and cress for a nose.

● **Left: Bean-mix salad:**
Right: Funny face salad

Bean-mix salad

SERVES 4

439 g (15½ oz) can red kidney beans,
*   drained*
198 g (7 oz) can sweetcorn, drained
50 g (2 oz) seedless raisins
1 small red pepper, seeded and diced
1 tbls finely chopped fresh parsley
1 tbls chopped salted peanuts
For the dressing
3 tbls vegetable oil
1 tbls vinegar
1 tbls Worcestershire sauce
1 tbls tomato ketchup
1 tbls soft light brown sugar

Place the beans, sweetcorn, raisins and red pepper in a bowl. Combine dressing ingredients, pour over salad; toss well. Add parsley and peanuts.

Pour the dressing over the bean mixture and toss well. Sprinkle with the parsley and peanuts before serving.

Lasagne with meatballs

SERVES 6

350 g (12 oz) lean minced beef
175 g (6 oz) cooked ham, minced
1 small onion, grated
1 tsp tomato purée
3 egg yolks
salt and pepper
vegetable oil, for frying
225 g (8 oz) lasagne sheets
For the sauce
50 g (2 oz) margarine or butter
50 g (2 oz) plain flour
750 ml (1¼ pints) milk
175 g (6 oz) Mozzarella, diced
4 tbls grated Parmesan cheese

In a bowl, mix the beef and ham with the onion, stir in the tomato purée and egg yolks and season to taste. Take heaped teaspoons of the mixture and shape into balls, using floured hands.

Heat the oil in a large frying pan, add the meatballs and fry for about 5 minutes, turning occasionally, until evenly brown. Remove with a slotted spoon and drain on kitchen paper.

Add the lasagne one sheet at a time to a large saucepan of boiling salted water and boil for 10-12 minutes, then drain the lasagne thoroughly.

Meanwhile, make the sauce. Melt the margarine in a saucepan, sprinkle in the flour and cook for 1-2 minutes, stirring constantly. Remove from the heat and gradually stir in the milk. Return to the heat and simmer for 2 minutes, stirring constantly until thickened and smooth. Stir in the Mozzarella and season to taste.

Heat the oven to 180°C, 350°F, Gas Mark 4.

Lay the lasagne sheets in a single layer on a wet tea towel, to prevent them from sticking together.

Spoon a little of the sauce over the base of a greased, large, shallow, rectangular ovenproof dish. Add a layer of lasagne, a few meatballs, and a little more of the sauce. Continue with alternate layers of lasagne, meatballs and sauce, finishing with a layer of sauce. Sprinkle the top with the grated Parmesan cheese.

Cook in the oven for 35-40 minutes until golden and bubbling. Serve hot.

• Left to right: Baked bean and bacon toasted sandwiches; Lasagne with meatballs; Sausage potato bake

Baked bean and bacon toasted sandwiches

SERVES 4

4-6 streaky bacon rashers, rinded
8 slices wholemeal bread
25 g (1 oz) butter, softened
1 tsp French mustard
8 tbls baked beans in tomato sauce

Heat the grill to high. Grill the bacon for about 3 minutes until crisp. Cool, then crumble.

Turn the grill to moderate. Spread the bread slices with the butter and French mustard. Spread 2 tbls baked beans on each of 4 bread slices and sprinkle a quarter of the bacon over each one. Top with remaining bread and press down.

Toast under grill for 1-2 minutes on each side. Cut into triangles to serve.

Sausage potato bake

SERVES 4

450 g (1 lb) pork sausages
6 tomatoes, skinned and halved
3 large potatoes, cooked
50 g (2 oz) margarine or butter
300 ml (½ pint) skimmed milk
salt and pepper
3 egg whites

Heat the oven to 200°C, 400°F, Gas Mark 6. Heat the grill to high.

Grill the sausages until golden brown. Drain on absorbent kitchen paper, then cut into chunks. Place in a flameproof casserole.

Arrange the tomatoes around the sausages, cut sides up. Mash the potatoes with the margarine and milk in a large bowl, to give a very soft consistency. Season to taste. Whisk the egg whites stiffly and fold lightly but thoroughly into the potato mixture.

Spoon the potato mixture around the sausages and tomatoes. Bake in the oven for about 20 minutes or until well risen and golden. Serve immediately.

Jiffy pizza

SERVES 4-6

For the base
225 g (8 oz) self-raising flour
1 tsp baking powder
½ tsp salt
25 g (1 oz) margarine or butter, diced
50 g (2 oz) Cheddar cheese, grated
150 ml (¼ pint) milk
For the topping
2 tbls vegetable oil
1 onion, finely chopped
2 tbls tomato purée
pinch of dried oregano
pinch of dried marjoram
salt and pepper
50 g (2 oz) Cheddar cheese, grated
50 g (2 oz) button mushrooms, sliced

Sift the flour with the baking powder
and salt into a mixing bowl. Add the
margarine and rub in with the fingertips until the mixture resembles coarse
breadcrumbs. Stir in the cheese, then
add the milk and mix to a rough dough.
Turn on to a floured surface and knead
lightly until smooth. Shape into a ball
and set aside while preparing the
pizza topping.

Heat the oven to 220°C, 425°F, Gas
Mark 7. Heat the oil in a small saucepan, add the onion and fry for 5
minutes until soft. Stir in the tomato
purée and herbs and season to taste.
Cook for a further 2 minutes, stirring
frequently, then remove from the heat.

Roll out the dough on a lightly floured
board or work surface to a 23 cm (9
inch) round. Transfer to a lightly
greased baking sheet and spread the
surface all over with the tomato mixture. Sprinkle with the grated cheese
and arrange the mushrooms over the
top of the pizza.

Bake in the oven for 20-25 minutes,
until well risen and golden.

Serving idea: Serve warm, cut into
wedges, with salad, or wrap wedges in
paper napkins for a TV snack.
Variation: Use sliced cooked sausage
instead of mushrooms.

Southern fried chicken

SERVES 4

4 chicken pieces, skinned
25 g (1 oz) plain flour, seasoned
2 eggs
150 ml (¼ pint) milk
175-225 g (6-8 oz) dry breadcrumbs
2 bananas, peeled and halved
*   lengthways*
4 streaky bacon rashers, rinded
vegetable oil, for deep frying
198 g (7 oz) can sweetcorn
watercress sprigs, to garnish

Pat the chicken pieces dry with absorbent kitchen paper. Dust the chicken
with the seasoned flour. Beat the eggs
with the milk in a shallow dish. Dip the

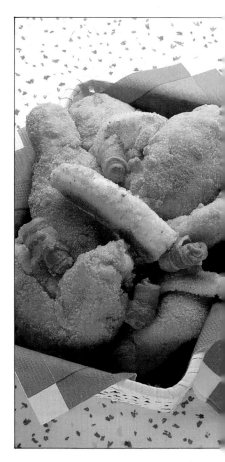

chicken pieces into the mixture, then coat them evenly with the bread-crumbs. Coat the halved bananas in the same way.

Heat the grill to moderate.

Lay the bacon rashers on a board and flatten and stretch them with the back of a knife. Cut each rasher in half lengthways, then roll up and secure with halved wooden cocktail sticks. Grill the bacon rolls, turning occasionally, for 10-15 minutes until cooked through and crisp. Drain on absorbent kitchen paper and keep hot on a heated serving dish.

Meanwhile heat the oil in a deep fat fryer to 190°C (375°F) or until a bread cube browns in 40 seconds. Fry the chicken pieces for 12-15 minutes, until golden and cooked through. Drain on absorbent kitchen paper and keep hot with the bacon. Fry the breaded bananas for 3-4 minutes, then drain on absorbent kitchen paper and arrange on the serving dish with the chicken and bacon.

Meanwhile, heat the sweetcorn in a saucepan. Drain and spoon around the bacon, chicken and bananas. Garnish with watercress sprigs and serve immediately.

Serving ideas: Accompany with individual bowls of mixed salad. Leftover chicken is a good lunchbox treat.

• Southern fried chicken; Jiffy pizza

Stuffed baked potatoes

SERVES 4

4 medium potatoes
vegetable oil, for brushing
25 g (1 oz) margarine or butter
1 onion, chopped
50 g (2 oz) mushrooms, chopped
salt and pepper
1 tbls sweet pickle
50 g (2 oz) cooked ham, chopped

Heat the oven to 200°C, 400°F, Gas Mark 6.

Prick the top of each potato with a fork and brush the skins lightly all over with oil. Bake in the oven for 45 minutes to 1 hour or until the potatoes are soft and cooked through.

Melt the margarine in a frying pan, add the onion and fry for about 5 minutes until softened. Add the mushrooms and fry for a further 2-3 minutes. Season to taste and stir in the pickle and ham.

Cut off the tops of the potatoes and scoop out the cooked flesh into a bowl, making sure you do not pierce the skins. Mash well and beat in the mushroom mixture. Spoon back into the potato skins. Return to the oven and bake for a further 10-15 minutes. Serve hot.

Serving idea: Serve with grilled tomatoes and coleslaw. Each potato may be garnished with a parsley sprig.
Variation: Grill 50 g (2 oz) bacon rashers, crumble and mix with the mushrooms and the ham. Sprinkle the stuffed potatoes with 50 g (2 oz) grated Cheddar cheese before returning to the oven to heat through.

Prawn jamboree

SERVES 4

4 bacon rashers, rinded and diced
1 small onion, finely sliced
½ green pepper, cored, seeded and
    diced
75 g (3 oz) long-grain rice
350 ml (12 fl oz) hot chicken stock
225 g (8 oz) ripe tomatoes, skinned,
    seeded and chopped
1 bay leaf
½ tsp chopped fresh basil
salt and pepper
275 g (10 oz) peeled prawns
1 tbls chopped fresh parsley (optional)

Fry the bacon in a large saucepan without added fat until crisp. Drain and set aside. Add the onion and green pepper to the pan and cook gently for about 5 minutes, or until softened.

Return the bacon to the pan and add the rice, stock, tomatoes, bay leaf and basil. Season to taste. Bring to the boil, cover and simmer for 15-20 minutes, or until the rice is tender.

Add the prawns and heat through gently. Discard the bay leaf and pile the prawn and rice mixture on to a heated serving dish. Sprinkle with parsley, if using, and serve immediately.

Surprise hamburger

SERVES 4

450 g (1 lb) minced beef
2 tbls finely chopped onion
1 tsp salt
¼ tsp pepper
50 g (2 oz) Cheddar cheese, grated

Heat the grill to moderate.

Put the beef, onion and seasoning into a bowl and mix well. Divide the mixture in half and shape into two 18 cm (7 inch) rounds.

Sprinkle the cheese evenly over one round, to within 1 cm (½ inch) of the edges. Cover with the second round and pinch the edges firmly to seal the filling inside.

Cook under the grill for about 6 minutes on each side, or until cooked through. Transfer to a heated serving dish and serve cut into 4 wedges.

Serving idea: Serve with chips or potato crisps, salad and burger relish.
Variations: Four individual hamburgers may be made by dividing the minced beef into 8 thin patties, adding 1 tbls grated cheese to half of them and topping and sealing with the remaining 4 patties. Grill for 4-5 minutes each side only. Garnish with tomato slices and onion rings. Mozzarella may be used instead of Cheddar.

● Surprise hamburger; Prawn jamboree;
Stuffed baked potatoes

Wholemeal vegetable samosas

MAKES 9

For the filling
3 carrots, diced
4 medium potatoes, diced
120 ml (4 fl oz) boiling water
½ tsp salt
1 tsp curry powder
5-6 fresh spinach leaves, finely
  chopped
For the pastry
350 g (12 oz) self-raising wholemeal
  flour
½ tsp salt
75 g (3 oz) margarine, diced
about 200 ml (⅓ pint) cold water
a little milk

Cook the carrots and potatoes in a saucepan with the boiling water, salt and curry powder for 10 minutes, shaking the pan occasionally.

Add the spinach leaves and simmer for a further 5 minutes, adding a little more boiling water if necessary.

Meanwhile, make the pastry. Sift the flour with the salt into a mixing bowl and tip in any bran left in the sieve. Add the margarine and rub in with the fingertips until the mixture resembles fine breadcrumbs. Stir in enough water to make a soft dough. Shape into a ball and divide into three equal portions. Heat the oven to 200°C, 400°F, Gas Mark 6.

Place one-third of the dough on a lightly floured work surface and roll out to an 18 × 23 cm (7 × 9 inch) rectangle. Spread one-third of the vegetable mixture down the centre of the rectangle. Moisten the edges with a little milk, then bring the long edges together and press together firmly to seal. Dust with a little flour and cut the rectangle into three triangles. Press edges to seal.

Repeat with remaining dough and vegetable mixture, to make 9 triangles in all. Place the samosas on a greased and floured baking sheet. Bake in the oven for 25 minutes until well risen and golden brown. Serve hot.

Sweetcorn fritters

MAKES ABOUT 12 FRITTERS

6 tbls plain wholemeal flour
1½ tsp baking powder
½ tsp salt
pepper
340 g (12 oz) can sweetcorn, drained
1 tsp clear honey
3 eggs, separated
150 g (5.29 oz) carton natural yoghurt
1 tbls chopped fresh parsley
a little vegetable oil, for frying
tomato slices, to garnish

Sift the flour with the baking powder and ½ tsp salt into a mixing bowl. Tip in any bran left in the sieve and season with pepper. Make a well in the centre and add the sweetcorn, honey, egg yolks, yoghurt and the parsley. Stir well to mix. Whisk the egg whites stiffly and fold them into the mixture.

Brush a frying pan with a little oil and heat gently. Drop in 2-3 tablespoonfuls batter and fry for 2 minutes or until the underside of fritters is brown. Turn and fry until other side is brown. Re-

● Left to right: Home-made fish cakes; Wholemeal vegetable samosas; Sweetcorn fritters

move from the pan and keep hot while frying the remaining fritters. Garnish with tomato slices and serve.

Home-made fish cakes

SERVES 4

350g (12 oz) cod fillet
1 bay leaf
2 medium potatoes
50g (2 oz) margarine or butter
1 small onion, finely chopped
salt and pepper
2 eggs, beaten
50g (2 oz) plain flour
100g (4 oz) fresh white breadcrumbs
vegetable oil, for deep frying
To garnish
8 lemon slices
8 tomato wedges
8 cooked peas

Place the cod in a saucepan, cover with water, add the bay leaf and poach gently for 10 minutes. Remove from the pan and discard the skin and any bones, then flake the flesh. Meanwhile, cook the potatoes in a saucepan of boiling salted water until tender. Drain well and mash with half the margarine. Melt the remaining margarine in a frying pan, add the onion and fry for 5 minutes until softened. In a bowl, beat together the fish, potato and onion and season to taste. Stir in half the beaten egg, to bind. Set aside in a cool place for 15-20 minutes to firm up.

Divide the mixture into 8 portions and mould into fish shapes. Coat first with flour, then with remaining beaten egg, then with breadcrumbs.

Heat the oil in a frying pan and add the fish cakes, a few at a time. Fry, turning occasionally, for 5-8 minutes, or until cooked through and golden. Drain on absorbent kitchen paper. Keep hot on a heated serving dish while frying the remaining fish cakes. Arrange the lemon slices on the fish to represent fins, the tomato to represent mouths and the peas to represent eyes.

Stuffed mushrooms

SERVES 4

8 large cup mushrooms
1/2 onion, finely chopped
25 g (1 oz) fresh white breadcrumbs
175 g (6 oz) sausagemeat
1 tbls chopped fresh parsley
1/2 tsp dried mixed herbs
salt and pepper
25 g (1 oz) margarine or butter, diced
To garnish
sweetcorn kernels
tomato quarters

Heat the oven to 190°C, 375°F, Gas Mark 5.
Remove the stalks from the mushrooms and finely chop the stalks. Place the stalks, onion, breadcrumbs, sausagemeat, parsley and mixed herbs in a bowl. Season to taste and stir well to mix, until thoroughly combined.
Place the mushroom caps, rounded side down, in a greased ovenproof dish. Spoon the stuffing mixture into the caps and dot with the margarine. Bake in the oven for about 25 minutes, or until the stuffing is cooked. Garnish with the sweetcorn and tomato and serve hot.

Serving idea: Serve the stuffed mushrooms on hot buttered toast.

Lamb and vegetable kebabs

SERVES 4

450 g/1 lb lean lamb, cubed
4 cherry tomatoes, or 2 small
  tomatoes, halved
8 button mushrooms
1 green pepper, cored, seeded and cut
  into squares
2 tbls olive oil
lemon slices, to garnish
freshly cooked rice, to serve

Divide the lamb, tomatoes, mushrooms and green pepper into 4 equal portions and thread them on to 4 greased kebab skewers, alternating the ingredients. Use wooden skewers for young children.
Heat the grill to moderate.
Brush a little oil over the kebabs and place them in the grill pan. Grill them for about 12-15 minutes, turning occasionally, or until all the ingredients are cooked through. Brush the meat with oil occasionally during cooking.
Serve the kebabs on a bed of rice, garnished with lemon slices.

Egg and chicken toasties

SERVES 4

50 g (2 oz) butter
4 large slices white bread, crusts
  removed
3 eggs
3 tablespoons milk
salt and pepper
100 g (4 oz) cooked chicken, chopped
1/2 red pepper, cored, seeded and
  finely diced
2 spring onions, finely chopped
25 g (1 oz) Cheddar cheese, grated

Heat the oven to 200°C, 400°F, Gas Mark 6.
Melt half the butter in a small saucepan. Brush both sides of each bread slice with the melted butter.
Line 4 individual Yorkshire pudding tins with the bread slices, pressing them down well but leaving the corners protruding. Bake in the oven for 15-20 minutes until crisp and golden.
Five minutes before the bread cases are ready, whisk the eggs with the milk in a bowl and season to taste with salt and pepper.
Melt the remaining butter in a saucepan and pour in the beaten egg mixture. Stir over gentle heat until the eggs are just set but still creamy.
Remove from the heat and stir in the remaining ingredients. Pile the mixture into the bread cases and serve immediately.

16

● Stuffed mushrooms; Lamb and vegetable kebabs; Egg and chicken toasties

Cheesy fish surprise

SERVES 4

2 plaice, divided into 8 fillets, skinned
100 g (4 oz) Cheddar cheese in one
piece
2 large eggs, beaten
225 (8 oz) fresh white breadcrumbs
vegetable oil, for deep frying

Rinse the plaice fillets and pat dry with absorbent kitchen paper.

Cut the cheese into 8 pieces, each long enough to fit just across the width of the plaice fillets. Place a piece of cheese on each fillet and roll it up, starting from the tail end.

Dip the plaice rolls first in beaten egg, then in breadcrumbs. Repeat, pressing the breadcrumbs on firmly to coat thoroughly.

Heat the oil in a deep fat fryer to 182°C (360°F) or until a bread cube browns in 60 seconds. Lower in the plaice rolls and fry for about 8 minutes until golden brown and crisp. Drain on absorbent kitchen paper and serve hot.

Puffy toasts

SERVES 4

4 slices wholemeal bread, crusts
removed
4 slices cooked ham
4 tomatoes, sliced
2 eggs, separated
1 tsp French mustard
25 g (1 oz) Edam cheese, grated
salt and pepper

Heat the oven to 180°C, 350°F, Gas Mark 4.

Lightly toast the bread on both sides. Place a ham slice on each piece of toast and top with the tomato slices. Place the toast slices on a greased baking sheet.

Beat the egg yolks with the mustard and cheese. Season to taste.

Whisk the egg whites stiffly, then fold into the egg yolk mixture, using a large metal spoon.

Spoon the soufflé mixture over the bread slices, dividing it equally among them. Bake in the oven for 15-20 minutes or until set.

Sardine bake

SERVES 4

12 small thin slices of bread
40 g (1½ oz) butter, softened
124 g (4⅜ oz) can sardines in tomato
* sauce*
2 tomatoes, skinned and chopped
salt and pepper
75 g (3 oz) Cheddar cheese, grated
2 large eggs
150 ml (¼ pint) milk
1 tomato, sliced, to garnish

Heat the oven to 200°C, 400°F, Gas Mark 6. Grease a 1.2 litre (2 pint) shallow pie dish.

Spread the bread slices with the butter.

Mash the sardines in their sauce and spread over the buttered bread slices. Cut each slice into 4 triangles.

Arrange a layer of the bread triangles to cover the base of the pie dish. Top with one-third of the chopped tomato, season to taste and top with one-quarter of the cheese. Make 2 more layers of bread triangles, tomato and cheese and top with a final layer of bread triangles.

Whisk the eggs with the milk and season to taste. Pour over the pie dish and sprinkle with remaining cheese.

Bake just above the centre of the oven for 25-30 minutes, until crisp and brown. Garnish with tomato slices.

● **Left: Puffy toasts;
Centre: Cheesy fish
surprise; Right:
Sardine bake**

Cottage pie

SERVES 4-6

1 tbls vegetable oil
1 onion, chopped
450g (1 lb) minced beef
198g (7 oz) can tomatoes
1 tbls tomato purée
salt and pepper
1 tbls cornflour
2 tbls water
25g (1 oz) margarine or butter
225g (8 oz) button mushrooms, sliced
1 tbls chopped fresh parsley
350g (12 oz) cooked potato, mashed
15g (½oz) Cheddar cheese, grated

Heat the oil in a large saucepan, add the onion and fry gently for about 5 minutes until softened. Add the minced beef and fry, stirring, until the meat is just brown. Stir in the tomatoes with their juice and the tomato purée and season to taste. Bring to the boil, then lower the heat, cover and simmer gently for 25 minutes, stirring occasionally. Adjust the seasoning to taste.

Mix the cornflour with the water to make a smooth paste and stir into the mixture. Simmer for a further 3-4 minutes, stirring from time to time.

Meanwhile, heat the oven to 190°C, 375°F, Gas Mark 5. Melt the margarine in a small saucepan, add the mushrooms and fry gently for 2-3 minutes. Stir in the parsley.

Spoon half the meat mixture into a 1.2 litre (2 pint) pie dish, then cover with the mushroom mixture. Spoon over the remaining meat mixture. Season the mashed potato and spread over the surface of the meat. Mark the potato decoratively with a fork and sprinkle

liberally with the grated cheese.

Bake in the oven for 35-40 minutes until the topping is golden. If liked, place the pie under a preheated hot grill just before serving to brown the potato topping lightly.

• Left: Hard-boiled eggs with vegetable soldiers; Right: Cottage pie

Hard-boiled eggs with vegetable soldiers

SERVES 4

4 eggs, hard-boiled
99g (3½oz) can tuna, drained and
   flaked
1 tsp tomato ketchup
2 tbls salad cream
salt and pepper
1 tbls chopped chives
1 carrot, cut into thin sticks
2 celery stalks, cut into thin lengths

Cut off the tops of the eggs and set aside. Carefully scoop out the egg yolks into a bowl. Add the tuna, tomato ketchup and salad cream and mash well together. Season to taste.

Using a teaspoon, fill the hard-boiled egg cavities with the tuna mixture and smooth over with a knife. Replace the reserved egg tops. Put the eggs into egg cups, on plates. Spoon a little of the remaining tuna mixture on to each of the serving plates and sprinkle with the chives.

Serve with carrot and celery sticks.

Tuna scramble rolls

MAKES 4

198g (7 oz) can tuna in oil, drained
1 tbls lemon juice
salt and pepper
1 tbls chopped fresh parsley
4 eggs
50g (2 oz) butter, softened
4 granary rolls

Mash the tuna in a bowl with the lemon juice and season to taste with salt and pepper. Stir in the parsley.

Beat the eggs in a bowl and season to taste. Melt half the butter in a small saucepan, add the egg mixture and stir over a gentle heat for about 5 minutes until the eggs are set but still creamy. Remove from the heat and set aside to cool.

Split the rolls and spread both halves of each with the remaining butter.

Spread the tuna mixture over the bottom half of each roll. Spoon on the scrambled egg and cover with top halves. Press down firmly. Wrap the rolls in cling film.

Variations: Floury white baps may be used instead of granary rolls.

For a hot variation for lunch or tea, stir the tuna mixture into the scrambled eggs as soon as they are cooked, and pile on to hot buttered toast.

Sardines canned in oil or tomato sauce may replace the tuna.

Cheese and raisin sandwiches

MAKES 4

4 large slices white bread
4 large slices wholemeal bread
50 g (2 oz) butter, softened
For the filling
175 g (6 oz) Cheddar or Edam cheese,
grated
25 g (1 oz) seedless raisins
1 tbls mayonnaise

Spread the bread slices with the butter.

Mix the cheese, raisins and mayonnaise together in a bowl and spread over the white bread slices. Cover with the wholemeal bread slices.

Press down firmly. Cut into halves or quarters and wrap in cling film.

Serving idea: Cut off the crusts if you are serving the sandwiches to younger children.
Variations: Tuna filling: Drain and flake a 99 g (3½ oz) can tuna. Mix with 1 tbls mayonnaise and 1 tbls chutney. Season to taste.
Liver sausage filling: Use 175 g (6 oz) sliced liver sausage and sprinkle with 2 tbls grated carrot and a little mustard and cress.
Prawn and egg filling: Mix 75 g (3 oz) chopped peeled prawns with 1 chopped hard-boiled egg and 2 tbls softened butter. Season to taste.
Cream cheese and pineapple filling: Mix 90 g (3½ oz) cream cheese with 227 g (8 oz) can drained crushed pineapple chunks.

Other popular fillings with children include: corned beef, tomato and mayonnaise; honey and nut; peanut butter and banana; chicken and pineapple; egg and cress; salmon and cucumber; scrambled egg and ham.

● Left: Cheese and raisin sandwiches;
Right: Tuna scramble rolls

23

Cornish pasties

SERVES 4

225 g (8 oz) plain flour
pinch of salt
100 g (4 oz) margarine or butter
2-3 tbls water
For the filling
175 g (6 oz) stewing beef, cooked and
*   very thinly sliced*
2 potatoes, coarsely grated
1 onion, finely chopped
salt and pepper
15 g (½ oz) unsalted butter, diced
1 egg, beaten, to glaze

Heat the oven to 200°C, 400°F, Gas Mark 6.

To make the pastry, sift the flour with the salt into a mixing bowl. Add margarine and rub in with the fingertips until the mixture resembles fine breadcrumbs. Add enough water to mix to a pliable dough.

Turn the dough on to a lightly floured work surface and roll out to about 5 mm (¼ inch) thick. Using a saucer as a guide, cut out 4 rounds.

To make the filling, mix the meat with the potatoes and onion and season to taste. Spoon a portion of the mixture on to each dough round, dividing it equally among them. Top each portion of filling with a piece of butter. Dampen the pastry edges with cold water and carefully draw up two edges to meet on top of the filling. Pinch and twist the pastry firmly together to make a neat fluted seam. Make a small slit in the side of each pasty.

Brush the pasties with the egg and place on a greased baking sheet. Bake in the oven for 10 minutes. Reduce the oven temperature to 180°C, 350°F, Gas Mark 4 and bake for a further 30 minutes, until golden brown.

Transfer to a wire rack and leave to cool completely. Wrap the pasties in foil or cling film.

Serving idea: Serve with a tomato, celery and cucumber salad, packed in a rigid container.

Cheese scones

MAKES 10

225 g (8 oz) self-raising flour
½ tsp salt
40 g (1½ oz) margarine
50 g (2 oz) Cheddar cheese, grated
2 tbls grated Parmesan cheese
1 tsp English mustard powder
about 150 ml (¼ pint) milk

Heat the oven to 230°C, 450°F, Gas Mark 8. Sift the flour with the salt into a mixing bowl. Add the margarine and rub in with the fingertips until the mixture resembles breadcrumbs. Mix the cheeses together and stir 50 g (2 oz) into

● Left: Cornish pasties; Right: Cheese scones

the bowl with the mustard. Stir in enough of the milk to make a soft dough.

Turn the dough on to a floured work surface and knead lightly. Roll out to 2 cm (¾ inch) thickness and cut into 10 rounds with a floured 5 cm (2 inch) plain cutter.

Place the dough rounds on a greased baking sheet and sprinkle with the remaining cheese. Bake in the oven for 10 minutes, or until well risen and golden brown. Transfer to a wire rack to cool.

Serving ideas: Serve the cheese scones split and buttered. Yeast extract, meat paste or cheese spread could be used to fill the buttered scones.

Variations: For plain scones, omit the cheeses and mustard. Increase the quantity of margarine to 50 g (2 oz) and the salt to 1 tsp. For sweet scones, use the plain scones variation and add 25 g (1 oz) caster sugar to the flour. Add 50 g (2 oz) sultanas, chopped dried dates or chopped dried apricots before adding the milk to the dry ingredients.

Chicken and ham pies

SERVES 4

175g (6oz) plain flour
pinch of salt
40g (1½oz) margarine or butter
40g (1½oz) lard
water, to mix
milk, to glaze
For the filling
15g (½oz) margarine or butter
15g (½oz) plain flour
6 tbls milk
40g (1½oz) cooked ham, chopped
75g (3oz) cooked chicken meat,
  chopped
salt and pepper
4 hard-boiled eggs

To make the filling, melt the margarine in a saucepan, sprinkle in the flour and cook for 1-2 minutes, stirring. Remove from the heat and gradually stir in the milk. Return to the heat and simmer for 2 minutes, stirring continuously. Remove from the heat and stir in the ham and chicken. Season to taste and set aside to cool.

Heat the oven to 220°C, 425°F, Gas Mark 7.

To make the pastry, sift the flour with the salt into a bowl. Add the margarine and lard and rub in with the fingertips until the mixture resembles fine breadcrumbs. Mix in enough water to make a pliable dough.

Turn the dough on to a lightly floured work surface and roll out fairly thinly.

Cut out 4 × 10 cm (4 inch) rounds and 4 × 9 cm (3½ inch) rounds. Reserve the trimmings.

Line the bases of 4 × 7.5 cm (3 inch) patty tins with the larger pastry circles. Spoon half the filling into the centre of each. Bury an egg in each portion of filling. Dampen the dough edges and carefully cover with the small rounds of dough. Press the edges well together and crimp.

Re-roll the pastry trimmings and cut out leaves. Brush with a little milk and use to decorate the tops of the pies. Brush the pastry all over with milk and make a small hole in the top of each.

Bake in the oven for 25-30 minutes, or until risen and golden brown. Cool thoroughly on a wire rack.

Serving idea: Accompany with coleslaw or a sweetcorn, apple and nut salad packed in a rigid container.

Variations: Diced grilled bacon or sliced cooked sausages may be used instead of the ham. Cooked turkey may replace the chicken. A little tomato purée may be added to the filling mixture.

Cheesy Scotch eggs

MAKES 4

450 g (1 lb) potatoes, cooked and mashed
100 g (4 oz) Cheddar cheese, grated
salt and pepper
4 hard-boiled eggs, shelled
1 egg, beaten
50 g (2 oz) dry breadcrumbs
vegetable oil, for deep frying

Beat the mashed potatoes and cheese until smooth, then season to taste with salt and pepper.

Divide the mixture into four portions and mould a portion around each egg, using floured hands. Dip the coated eggs in beaten egg and coat with the breadcrumbs.

Heat the oil in a deep fat fryer to 190°C (375°F) or until a bread cube browns in 40 seconds. Fry the eggs for about 5 minutes, or until golden brown and crisp. Drain on absorbent kitchen paper and allow to cool completely.

Serving ideas: Accompany with salad, or with tomatoes and cold cooked sausages, for a more substantial meal.
Variation: Scotch eggs are more conventionally made with sausagemeat to wrap around the eggs. Use 225 g (8 oz) pork sausagemeat instead of the potatoes and cheese.

● Left: Chicken and ham pies;
Right: Cheesy Scotch eggs

Waldorf salad

SERVES 4-6

2 tbls lemon juice
1 tsp caster sugar
150 ml (¼ pint) thick mayonnaise
450 g (1 lb) red dessert apples, cored
   but unpeeled
½ head celery, chopped
50 g (2 oz) shelled walnuts, chopped
1 lettuce, separated into leaves
a few walnut halves, to garnish

In a bowl, mix together the lemon juice, sugar and 1 tbls of the mayonnaise. Slice one apple thinly and dice the remainder. Dip the apple slices in the mayonnaise dressing and set aside. Add the diced apple to the remaining dressing, turn to coat thoroughly, cover and set aside for 30 minutes.

Add the celery and walnuts to the diced apple with the remaining mayonnaise and stir well to mix. Line a large rigid container with the lettuce leaves, pile the salad in the centre and arrange the apple slices and walnut halves on top.

Serving ideas: Serve with sliced tongue, ham, beef or chicken.
Variation: Other nuts, such as peanuts, may replace the walnuts.

Frankfurter and potato salad

SERVES 4

750 g (1½ lb) new potatoes, scrubbed
salt
3 tbls vegetable oil
1 tbls vinegar
pinch of sugar
1 tsp lemon juice
1 small bunch spring onions, chopped
4 frankfurters, cut into 1 cm (½ inch)
   chunks
4 tbls salad cream
1 tsp burger mustard (optional)

● Left: Frankfurter and potato salad;
Centre: Waldorf salad; Right: Celery
boats

Celery boats

MAKES ABOUT 24

1 head of celery
50 g (2 oz) peanut butter
50 g (2 oz) full fat soft cheese
25 g (1 oz) peeled prawns, chopped
50 g (2 oz) smooth liver pâté
50 g (2 oz) Cheddar cheese, grated
1 tbls mango chutney, chopped
extra peeled prawns, to garnish

Cook the potatoes for 10-12 minutes in boiling, salted water, until just tender, then drain and cut into 2 cm (¾ inch) chunks. Place in a large bowl.

Mix together the oil, vinegar, sugar and lemon juice and pour over the hot potatoes. Toss well and set aside for 30-40 minutes.

Mix together the onions and frank-furters. Combine the salad cream and mustard, if using, and stir into the frankfurter mixture. Add to the pota-toes and stir well to mix, making sure all the ingredients are thoroughly coated with dressing.

Serving idea: Pack in rigid containers for a picnic or school lunch.
Variation: Use sliced cold cooked pork sausages instead of frankfurters.

Separate the celery into sticks, wash and scrub well. Trim both ends. Cut into 4 cm (1½ inch) lengths, to make boats.

Using a teaspoon, fill 6 of the celery boats with peanut butter. Mix the soft cheese and prawns together and use to fill another 6 in the same way. Spread the pâté into half the remaining celery boats. Combine the grated cheese and chutney and use to fill the remainder. Garnish each filled celery boat with a prawn, then wrap in foil.

Bacon and egg pie

SERVES 4-6

225 g (8 oz) plain flour
pinch of salt
65 g (2½ oz) margarine, diced
65 g (2½ oz) lard, diced
2-3 tbls cold water
a little beaten egg, to glaze
For the filling
4 streaky bacon rashers, rinded and
*   chopped*
50 g (2 oz) mushrooms, sliced
4 eggs
5 tbls milk
salt and pepper
1 tsp dried thyme
1 tbls chopped fresh parsley
2 tomatoes, sliced

To make the pastry, sift the flour with the salt into a mixing bowl. Add the margarine and lard and rub in with the fingertips until the mixture resembles fine breadcrumbs. Mix in enough water to make a pliable dough. Cut the dough in half.

Heat the oven to 200°C, 400°F, Gas Mark 6.

Turn half the dough on to a lightly floured work surface and roll out fairly thinly. Use to line a 20 cm (8 inch) sandwich tin. Roll out the remaining dough and cut out a 20 cm (8 inch) circle for a lid. Reserve the pastry trimmings.

Scatter the bacon over the pastry base and top with the mushrooms. Whisk the eggs together with the milk. Season to taste and add the thyme and parsley. Pour over the bacon and mushroom mixture and top with tomato slices.

Dampen the dough edges and cover with the lid, pressing together firmly to seal. Trim and scallop the edges.

Re-roll the pastry trimmings and cut out leaves. Brush with a little milk and use to decorate the top of the pie. Brush the pastry all over with milk and make a small hole in the top.

Bake the pie in the oven for 10 minutes, then reduce the oven temperature to 180°C, 350°F, Gas Mark 4 and bake for a further 30 minutes, until well-risen and golden.

Leave to cool slightly, then carefully turn out on to a wire rack and allow to cool completely. Wrap whole or in slices in foil.

Serving ideas: Serve with potato salad packed in a rigid container. For eating at home, serve hot with buttered noodles and sliced runner beans.

Peanut cheese dip

SERVES 4-6

25 g (1 oz) margarine or butter
2 tbls plain flour
300 ml (½ pint) milk
175 g (6 oz) Cheddar cheese, grated
3 tbls salted peanuts, chopped
2 celery sticks, finely chopped
½ tsp English mustard
salt and pepper

Melt the margarine in a saucepan, stir in the flour and cook for 1-2 minutes, stirring. Remove from the heat and gradually stir in the milk. Return to the heat and simmer for 2 minutes, stirring continuously, until thickened and smooth. Remove from the heat, add the cheese and stir until melted.

Reserve 2 tsp of the peanuts and stir the remainder with the celery and mustard into the cheese sauce. Season to taste. Allow to cool, then turn into a rigid container. Sprinkle over the reserved peanuts.

Serving ideas: Use celery or carrot sticks, twiglets or savoury crackers to dunk in the dip.

• Peanut cheese dip; Bacon and egg pie

Floating islands

SERVES 4-6

2 egg whites
100g (4oz) caster sugar, plus 2 tbls
600ml (1 pint) milk
3 eggs
1 tbls cornflour
a few drops of vanilla essence
To decorate
25g (1 oz) blanched almonds
25g (1 oz) caster sugar

Whisk the egg whites stiffly in a clean dry bowl. Whisk in 100g (4oz) sugar, a tablespoonful at a time, until very stiff and glossy.

Heat the milk and 2 tbls sugar in a saucepan to simmering point. To shape the 'islands', take a tablespoon of meringue and use a second tablespoon to form a smooth egg shape. Carefully slide 4 'islands' into the milk. Simmer very gently for 3 minutes, then carefully remove with a slotted spoon and drain on a clean tea towel. Repeat twice more, to make 12 meringue 'islands' in all.

Beat the eggs with the cornflour in a bowl and stir in the hot milk with the vanilla essence. Strain into a clean saucepan and cook gently, stirring constantly, until the custard is thick enough to coat the back of a wooden spoon. Remove from the heat, allow to cool slightly and pour into a glass serving dish.

Place the almonds and sugar in a small saucepan. Heat gently without stirring until the sugar caramelizes and turns brown. Pour evenly over a greased baking sheet and set aside until cold. Remove from the baking sheet and chop fairly finely.

Arrange the meringue 'islands' on the surface of the custard. Sprinkle the meringue 'islands' with the almond caramel and serve immediately.

Serving ideas: An attractive dessert to serve at a children's party or when friends come round for lunch or tea.

● Banana lollies; Floating islands

Banana lollies

MAKES 12

6 large firm bananas, peeled
12 wooden skewers or thin lolly sticks
350 g (12 oz) plain or milk chocolate,
  broken into pieces
15 g (½ oz) butter
coloured hundreds and thousands or
  chocolate vermicelli, to decorate

Cut each banana in half crossways. Fix each banana half on to a wooden skewer so that the skewer penetrates at least 5 cm (2 inches) into the banana. Place the bananas on a sheet of foil and place in the freezer or ice compartment of the refrigerator for 1 hour.

Place the chocolate and butter in a heatproof bowl set over a saucepan of simmering water. Stir until the chocolate has melted.

Remove one banana half at a time from the freezer, hold it over the bowl and spoon the melted chocolate over the banana to coat evenly. The chocolate coating will begin to set immediately on the bananas.

Sprinkle the chocolate-coated bananas with hundreds and thousands and lay carefully on a sheet of lightly oiled greaseproof paper, or push the sticks into a block of flower-arranging oasis. Leave to set completely, then wrap lightly in foil or freezer wrap, and return to the freezer or ice compartment of the refrigerator. Serve ice-cold, straight from the freezer.

Serving ideas: Serve as a dessert, a party sweet or instead of an ice lolly.
Variations: Decorate the bananas in different ways, such as making a face with sweets or using icing to pipe on a child's name or a number decoration for a birthday party. If using icing, allow the chocolate coating to set first.

Pancake parcels

SERVES 4

For the batter
100g (4 oz) plain flour
¼ tsp salt
1 egg
300 ml (½ pint) milk
vegetable oil, for frying
For the filling
3 bananas
3 tbls lemon juice
2 tbls apricot jam
For the sauce
4 tbls undiluted orange squash
2 tbls soft light brown sugar
25 g (1 oz) margarine or butter
½ tsp ground cinnamon (optional)
ice cream, to serve

Sift the flour with the salt into a mixing bowl and make a well in the centre. Add the egg, then gradually beat in the milk with a wooden spoon, drawing in the flour from the sides to make a smooth batter.

Heat a little oil in a frying pan until very hot, making sure the base and sides are evenly coated, and pour off any excess. Pour in a few spoonfuls of batter, tilting the pan so that it spreads out evenly, and cook over a high heat for about 2 minutes until golden brown. Turn or toss the pancake and cook the underside until golden brown. Remove from the pan and keep hot while frying the remaining batter in the same way, to make 8 pancakes in all. Stack the pancakes as they are cooked, with a disc of greaseproof paper between each.

● Left: Pancake parcels; Right: Tropical knickerbocker glories

Tropical knickerbocker glories

SERVES 4

about 600 ml (1 pint) or 1 family block
    bought mango fruit cocktail ice
    cream
300 ml (½ pint) raspberry sorbet
2 kiwi fruits, peeled and chopped
1 mango, peeled, stoned and chopped
For the orange syrup
150 ml (¼ pint) fresh orange juice
25 g (1 oz) sugar
To decorate
142 ml (5 fl oz) carton whipping
    cream, whipped
25 g (1 oz) flaked almonds, toasted

Make the orange syrup: put the orange juice and sugar into a small saucepan, bring to the boil and boil for 5-10 minutes until reduced and syrupy. Allow to cool, then chill in the refrigerator.

Remove the ice cream and sorbet from the freezer and allow to soften in the refrigerator for 45 minutes. Place 4 sundae glasses in the refrigerator and chill.

Place a scoop of ice cream in the base of each chilled glass, then sprinkle with a little kiwi fruit. Top with a scoop of sorbet, then chopped mango. Repeat until the glass is almost full.

Pour over the orange syrup, top each knickerbocker glory with a swirl of whipped cream and sprinkle with almonds. Serve immediately, with long handled spoons.

Serving idea: Decorate each knickerbocker glory with a fan wafer.

Variations: Use pineapple or strawberry sorbet and replace the kiwi fruit with chopped pineapple or sliced strawberries.

To make the filling, peel the bananas, then mash the flesh with the lemon juice and jam. Spoon a portion of the filling into the centre of each pancake, dividing it equally among them, then fold the sides of each pancake around the filling to make 'parcels'.

To make the sauce, make the orange squash up to 150 ml (¼ pint) with water, then pour into a large frying pan. Add the sugar, margarine and cinnamon, if using. Bring to the boil, stirring constantly, and boil for 5 minutes until syrupy, then reduce the heat.

Arrange the pancake parcels in a single layer in the pan, then heat through for about 10 minutes, spooning the sauce over the pancakes occasionally. Serve hot, with ice cream slices on the side.

Individual cherry puddings

SERVES 6

6 tbls golden syrup
100 g (4 oz) glacé cherries
75 g (3 oz) plain flour
1 tsp baking powder
pinch of salt
75 g (3 oz) fresh white breadcrumbs
75 g (3 oz) shredded suet
40 g (1½ oz) caster sugar
1 egg, beaten
6-8 tbls milk

Put 1 tbls golden syrup in the bottom of each of 6 buttered individual dariole moulds. Cut about 18 cherries in half, then place them cut sides uppermost in the bottom of the moulds. Chop the remaining cherries roughly and set aside while making the sponge.

Sift the flour with the baking powder and salt into a mixing bowl. Add the breadcrumbs, suet and sugar and stir well to mix, then stir in the reserved chopped cherries and the egg. Gradually add enough milk to give a soft dropping consistency, beating well between each addition. Spoon the mixture into the moulds, dividing it equally among them.

Cover the tops of the puddings with rounds of buttered greaseproof paper. Cover the tops of the moulds with pleated foil, to allow for expansion during steaming. Tie securely round the edge of each mould with string.

Place the moulds in the top of a steamer or double boiler, or in a saucepan with boiling water poured in halfway up the sides of the moulds. Cover and steam for 1 hour, topping up with more boiling water as necessary.

Lift out the puddings and remove the foil and greaseproof paper. Leave until cool enough to handle, then turn the puddings out on to a heated serving dish. Serve hot.

Serving idea: Serve with pouring custard, single cream or scoops of vanilla ice cream.

Chinese toffee apples

SERVES 4-6

4 large, firm dessert apples, cored and peeled
4 tbls plain flour
1 tbls cornflour
2 egg whites
vegetable oil, for deep frying
100 g (4 oz) sugar
2 tbls water
1 tbls lard
1 tbls sesame seeds

Cut each apple into eighths. Dust the apple pieces with a little of the flour.

Mix the remaining flour with the

cornflour in a bowl and whisk in the egg whites to make a smooth batter.

Heat the oil in a deep fat fryer to 190°C (375°F), or until a bread cube browns in 40 seconds. Dip each apple piece in the batter and deep fry for about 3 minutes until crisp and golden. Remove with a slotted spoon and drain thoroughly on absorbent kitchen paper.

Place the sugar and water in a large saucepan and stir over a low heat until the sugar is dissolved. Add the lard, increase the heat and continue stirring until the sugar caramelizes and turns brown. Add the apple pieces, turn to coat in the caramel, and stir in the sesame seeds. Transfer to a serving bowl.

Place a bowl of cold water on the table. Provide cocktail sticks for spearing the apple pieces and dipping into the water to harden the toffee.

Serving ideas: These Chinese toffee apples are ideal fun food. Scrve them at a Hallowe'en party as an alternative to bobbing for apples, or make them on a rainy afternoon during school holidays.

● Left: Individual cherry puddings; Right: Chinese toffee apples

Orange and yoghurt mould

SERVES 4-6

*thinly pared rind and juice of 4 large
   oranges*
*150 ml (¼ pint) water, plus a little
   extra*
100 g (4 oz) caster sugar
15 g (½ oz) sachet powdered gelatine
3 tbls lemon juice
150 g (5.29 oz) carton natural yoghurt
To decorate (optional)
*2 small oranges, peeled and sliced
   into rounds*
*25-50 g (1-2 oz) almonds, slivered or
   chopped*

Make up the orange juice to 300 ml (½
pint) with water if necessary and place
in a saucepan with the rind, 150 ml (¼
pint) water and sugar.

Stir over a low heat until the sugar
has dissolved. Bring slowly to the boil,
then remove from the heat and set
aside to infuse for at least 10 minutes.

Meanwhile, sprinkle the gelatine
over the lemon juice in a small heatproof bowl and leave for a few minutes
until spongy. Stand the bowl in a saucepan of hot water and stir over gentle
heat until the gelatine has dissolved.

Strain the orange juice mixture into
a bowl and stir in the liquid gelatine.
Leave until on the point of setting, then
fold in the yoghurt. Pour into a wetted
600 ml (1 pint) mould, then chill in the

● Orange and yoghurt mould; Ice cream crunch

refrigerator for at least 4 hours or until set firm.

Turn the jelly out on to a serving platter and decorate with orange slices and almonds, if using. Serve the orange and yoghurt mould well chilled.

Ice cream crunch

SERVES 4-6

4 egg yolks
100 g (4 oz) caster sugar
450 ml (¾ pint) milk
2-3 drops vanilla essence
50 g (2 oz) dry wholemeal
  breadcrumbs
142 ml (5 fl oz) carton whipping cream

Beat the egg yolks with the sugar in a heatproof bowl until the mixture is pale and creamy.

Place the milk and vanilla essence in a saucepan and heat to just below boiling point. Remove from the heat and slowly pour the hot milk on to the yolk mixture, stirring constantly.

Set the bowl over a saucepan of simmering water, making sure the base does not touch the water, and cook gently for about 10 minutes, stirring constantly with a wooden spoon, until the custard is thickened and coats the back of the spoon.

Remove from the heat and strain the custard into a bowl. Whisk until cool, to prevent a skin forming.

Pour the custard into a rigid container, cover and freeze for about 1½ hours or until beginning to set round the edges.

Meanwhile, lightly toast the breadcrumbs under a preheated low grill, turning them with a fork to ensure that they toast evenly. Remove from the heat and set aside to cool.

Whip the cream until it forms soft peaks. Transfer the partially frozen custard to a large bowl and beat well. Lightly fold in the cream and breadcrumbs, using a large metal spoon. Return to the container, cover and freeze for 1 further hour, then transfer to the bowl and beat thoroughly again, to break up all the ice crystals.

Cover the container and freeze until firm.

Serving ideas: Serve with wafers or crisp sweet biscuits. Or serve scoops of the ice cream in cones, decorated with pieces of chocolate flake.

Fruity yoghurt whips

SERVES 4

2 egg whites
2 tbls soft light brown sugar
2 × 150 g (5.29 oz) cartons natural
  yoghurt
2 tbls mixed dried fruit
1 tbls cut mixed peel
2 tbls chopped hazelnuts
1 large banana, peeled and chopped
1 tsp lemon juice

Whisk the egg whites stiffly. Add the sugar a tablespoon at a time, whisking again after each addition until stiff and glossy. Gently fold in the yoghurt, using a large metal spoon.

Fold in the dried fruit, peel and most of the nuts, reserving a few to decorate. Toss the banana in the lemon juice and fold in.

Divide the mixture among 4 serving glasses and sprinkle each one with a few of the reserved nuts. Chill in the refrigerator for a few minutes before serving.

Serving idea: Serve with sponge finger biscuits.
Variations: Flavoured yoghurt, such as hazelnut and peach, may replace the plain yoghurt.

● **Fruity yoghurt whip; Mandarin jelly castles**

Mandarin jelly castles

SERVES 4

135 g (4¾ oz) packet tangerine jelly, cubed
125 ml (4 fl oz) boiling water
425 g (15 oz) can semolina pudding
To decorate
4 tablespoons desiccated coconut
312 g (11 oz) can mandarin orange segments, drained
crystallized angelica

Rinse out four 150 ml (¼ pint) moulds or yoghurt cartons with cold water.

Place the jelly in a small saucepan with the boiling water and stir over very low heat until the jelly is dissolved. Remove from the heat and set aside to cool for 5 minutes.

Whisk the semolina pudding into the jelly until evenly blended. Divide the mixture equally among the wetted moulds, cover with cling film and chill in the refrigerator for 2 hours, or until the jellies are set.

Unmould the jellies into individual glass serving dishes. Sprinkle the tops and sides of the jellies with coconut. Arrange all but 4 of the mandarin orange segments around the base of the jellies. Decorate the top of each jelly with a mandarin orange segment and a piece of angelica. Serve chilled.

Variation: For Raspberry jelly castles, use a raspberry jelly and fresh or thawed frozen raspberries instead of mandarin orange segments.

Raspberry banana boats

SERVES 4

225 g (8 oz) raspberries, thawed if
  frozen
2 tbls icing sugar, sifted
142 ml (5 fl oz) carton whipping cream
4 bananas
300 ml (½ pint) vanilla ice cream
2 tbls chopped mixed nuts

Reserve 4 of the raspberries for decoration. Press the remaining raspberries through a sieve, into a saucepan. Add the icing sugar and stir over gentle heat until dissolved. Remove from the heat, cool slightly, then chill.

Stir half the cream into the raspberry purée. Whip the remaining cream until stiff.

Peel and halve the bananas lengthways, then place 2 halves in each of 4 individual shallow dessert bowls. Top each serving with a scoop of ice cream, then drizzle over the cream and raspberry mixture. Top each boat with a whirl of whipped cream, sprinkle with nuts and decorate with the raspberries. Serve immediately.

Serving idea: Decorate the boats with wafers, to look like sails.
Variations: For a more economical version, omit the whipped cream.

42

Fresh fruit salad

● Left: Raspberry banana boats;
Right: Fresh fruit salad

SERVES 6

1 ogen melon
2 oranges, peeled and segmented
2 apples, cored and sliced
2 pears, peeled, cored and chopped
100 g (4 oz) seedless grapes
½ yellow grapefruit, peeled and
  segmented
½ pink grapefruit, peeled and
  segmented
1 kiwi fruit, peeled and sliced
225 g (½ lb) strawberries, hulled and
  halved
1-2 tbls Barbados sugar or clear honey
juice of 1 lemon

Cut the melon in half and use a scoop to remove the flesh. Mix all the fruit together in a serving dish. Stir the sugar or honey into the lemon juice and pour it over the fruit.

Serving idea: Serve with natural yoghurt, cream, or ice cream. To obtain the maximum benefit of the high vitamin C content of the fresh fruit the salad should be prepared just before eating.
Variation: Fresh peaches, apricots and cherries may also be included.

43

Crispy crackles

MAKES 16

50 g (2 oz) butter
2 tbls golden syrup
*50 g (2 oz) drinking chocolate powder,
    sifted*
50 g (2 oz) cornflakes

Place the butter and golden syrup in a
saucepan and stir over a low heat until
melted. Remove from the heat and stir
in the drinking chocolate and cornflakes. Mix well to coat the cornflakes
thoroughly in the chocolate syrup
mixture.

Using a teaspoon, spoon the mixture
into paper sweet cases and leave until
thoroughly set.

Serving idea: These teatime favourites
are popular at children's parties.
Variations: Use bran flakes instead of
the cornflakes. Add 1-2 tbls raisins or
chopped glacé cherries to the mixture.

Flapjacks

MAKES ABOUT 16

100 g (4 oz) demerara sugar
100 g (4 oz) margarine or butter
3 tbls clear honey
175 g (6 oz) porridge oats
50 g (2 oz) desiccated coconut
1 tsp baking powder
1/2 tsp salt
1 egg, beaten

Heat the oven to 180°C, 350°F, Gas Mark 4. Grease a shallow 20 cm (8 inch) square baking tin.

Place the sugar with the margarine and honey in a saucepan and stir over a low heat until melted. Remove from the heat and stir in all the remaining ingredients. Stir well to mix.

Spoon the mixture into the prepared tin, spread out evenly and press down with the back of a spoon. Bake in the oven for 20-30 minutes, or until golden and firm to the touch.

Remove from the oven and leave to cool in the tin for 5 minutes, then cut into squares and leave until completely cold. Loosen each square with a palette knife and lift carefully from the tin.

Serving ideas: Serve for tea or include in a packed lunch box.

● **Left: Crispy crackles;
Right: Flapjacks**

Peach melba cake

MAKES AN 18 cm (7 inch) CAKE

2 eggs
a few drops of vanilla essence
50 g (2 oz) caster sugar
50 g (2 oz) plain flour
For the topping
225 g (8 oz) raspberries, thawed if
    frozen
3 tbls caster sugar
284 ml (10 fl oz) carton double cream
2 tbls milk
50 g (2 oz) flaked almonds, toasted
1 fresh peach, peeled, stoned and
    sliced, or 8 canned peach slices
2 tbls sugar (optional)
1 tbls lemon juice (optional)

Heat the oven to 190°C, 375°F, Gas Mark 5. Grease and flour an 18 cm (7 inch) square cake tin.

Whisk the eggs with the vanilla essence and sugar in a bowl until thick and pale. Sift half the flour into the mixture and fold it in, using a large metal spoon. Sift and fold in the remaining flour. Pour into the prepared tin.

Bake the cake in the oven for 20-30 minutes until well risen and golden and a skewer inserted into the centre comes out clean. Allow to cool slightly in the tin, then turn out on to a wire tray and leave to cool completely.

Trim the cake edges neatly and cut in half crossways. Reserve half of the raspberries for decoration. Press the remainder through a sieve into a bowl. Stir in the caster sugar.

Spread three-quarters of the raspberry purée on one half of the cake.

Whip the cream and the milk together until it forms soft peaks. Place one-third in a piping bag fitted with a medium star nozzle. Spread one-third of the remainder over both halves of the cake, then sandwich the two together with the raspberry purée and cream layer in the centre.

Spread the sides of the cake with the remaining cream, then press on the almonds, using a palette knife.

Pipe rosettes of cream down each long side of the top of the gâteau and chill in the refrigerator until ready to serve.

If using a fresh peach, place the sugar, lemon juice and a little water in a small saucepan and stir over gentle heat until dissolved. Add the peach slices and cook for 3 minutes. Remove with a slotted spoon, drain on absorbent kitchen paper and chill in the refrigerator.

Arrange the peach slices in a row down the centre of the cake. Using a teaspoon, drizzle a little of the remaining raspberry purée over each peach slice. Decorate the gâteau with the reserved raspberries.

Serving ideas: Serve for tea or as a dessert, or as an alternative to a conventional birthday cake.

Lemon surprise cake

MAKES AN 18 cm (7 inch) CAKE

175 g (6 oz) margarine or butter
175 g (6 oz) caster sugar
4 tsp grated lemon rind
6 tbls lemon juice
3 eggs
175 g (6 oz) self-raising flour, sifted
For the filling
25 g (1 oz) margarine or butter
25 g (1 oz) demerara sugar
25 g (1 oz) Brazil nuts, finely chopped
75 g (3 oz) sultanas
25 g (1 oz) glacé cherries
4 tsp grated lemon rind
pinch of grated nutmeg
To decorate
sifted icing sugar
sugared lemon halves

Heat the oven to 180°C, 350°F, Gas Mark 4. Grease an 18 cm (7 inch) cake tin and line the base with greased greaseproof paper.

To make the filling, melt the margarine in a small saucepan, then add the demerara sugar and stir until the sugar is dissolved. Remove from heat and stir in the nuts, sultanas, cherries,

46

• Lemon surprise cake; Peach melba cake

lemon rind and nutmeg. Set aside.

Cream the margarine and sugar in a mixing bowl until light and fluffy, then add the lemon rind. Beat the lemon juice with the eggs, then stir half into the creamed mixture. Fold in half the flour, then fold in remainder alternately with remaining egg mixture.

Spoon half the sponge mixture into the prepared tin. Sprinkle half the filling mixture over the top. Spoon over the remaining sponge mixture and

sprinkle with the remaining filling. (The fruit will sink during baking.)

Bake the cake in the oven for 1¼-1½ hours, until well risen and golden and a skewer inserted into the centre comes out clean. Cover with foil towards the end of baking time, to avoid burning. Remove from oven and allow to cool for 5 minutes in tin, then turn out on to wire rack, remove lining paper, and cool completely. Dredge with icing sugar and decorate with lemon halves.

Caramel shortbreads ✓

MAKES ABOUT 16

150 g (5 oz) butter
100 g (4 oz) caster sugar
275 g (10 oz) plain flour
For the filling
100 g (4 oz) butter or margarine
100 g (4 oz) caster sugar
2 tbls golden syrup
1 large can condensed milk
    (equivalent to 1.1 litres (1⅛ pints)
    skimmed milk)
100 g (4 oz) plain chocolate, broken
    into pieces, for the topping

Heat the oven to 180°C, 350°F, Gas Mark 4. Grease a 30 × 23 cm (12 × 9 inch) Swiss roll tin.

Cream the butter with the sugar in a bowl. Gradually work in the flour, beat-ing with a wooden spoon or electric hand-held beater. Press the mixture into the prepared tin.

Bake the shortbread in the oven for 15-20 minutes, until golden. Remove from the oven. Cool completely.

To make the filling, place the butter, sugar, syrup and condensed milk in a saucepan and heat gently until the sugar has dissolved, stirring occa-sionally. Increase the heat and boil for 5 minutes, stirring continuously. Re-move from heat, leave to cool for 1 min-ute, then pour on to the cooled short-bread base in the tin. Leave to set.

Place the chocolate in a small heat-proof bowl set over a saucepan of hot water and stir over gentle heat until melted. Spread over the set filling. Mark into fingers or squares and leave to cool and set completely before cutting into pieces and removing from the tin.

Jammy buns

MAKES 12

225 g (8 oz) self-raising flour
pinch of salt
pinch of mixed spice
50 g (2 oz) butter, diced
50 g (2 oz) caster sugar
1 egg, beaten
2 tbls milk
2 tbls strawberry jam
1 tbls sugar

Sift the flour with the salt and mixed spice into a mixing bowl. Add the butter and rub in with the fingertips until the mixture resembles fine breadcrumbs. Stir in the sugar, then add the egg and enough milk to make a firm dough. Turn on to a lightly floured work surface and knead lightly until smooth.

● Left: Jammy buns;
Right: Caramel shortbreads

Divide the dough into 12 pieces and roll them into balls. Make a hole in each and spoon in ½ tsp jam, pinching the opening together firmly to seal.

Place the buns, sealed side down, on a greased baking sheet and sprinkle with the sugar. Bake in the oven for 10 minutes, or until golden brown. Transfer to a wire rack and leave until thoroughly cool.

Variations: Use a few drops of vanilla essence instead of the mixed spice. Raspberry, blackcurrant or plum jam may be used instead of strawberry. Lemon curd may replace the jam.

Iced cup cakes

MAKES 20

150 g (5 oz) self-raising flour
100 g (4 oz) soft margarine
100 g (4 oz) caster sugar
2 eggs
2-3 drops vanilla essence
For the icing
225 g (8 oz) icing sugar
2-3 tablespoons warm water
few drops of food colouring (optional)
glacé cherries, hundreds and
    thousands, orange and lemon
    slices, chocolate vermicelli, tiny
    sweets to decorate

● Below: Iced cup cakes;
Right: Brownies

Heat the oven to 180°C, 350°F, Gas Mark 4.

Stand 20 paper cake cases on a baking sheet.

Sift the flour into a mixing bowl. Add the margarine, sugar, eggs and vanilla, then beat with a wooden spoon for 1-2 minutes, until evenly blended.

Using a teaspoon, divide the mixture equally among the paper cases. Bake in the oven for about 15 minutes until golden and springy to the touch. Transfer the cakes in their cases to a wire rack and leave to cool completely.

To make the icing, sift the icing sugar into a bowl and mix in enough water to give a smooth coating consistency. Divide the icing into 3 or 4 portions, if liked, and colour each with different food colouring.

Spread the icing over the tops of the cakes, decorate while the icing is still soft, then leave until the icing is set.

Brownies

MAKES ABOUT 16

100 g (4 oz) butter
100 g (4 oz) plain chocolate, broken
   into pieces
100 g (4 oz) soft light brown sugar
100 g (4 oz) self-raising flour
pinch of salt
2 eggs, beaten
50 g (2 oz) walnuts, coarsely chopped
1-2 tbls milk

Place the butter and chocolate pieces in a heatproof bowl set over a saucepan of hot water. Stir over gentle heat until the chocolate is melted. Remove the bowl from the heat and stir in the sugar. Set aside to cool.

Heat the oven to 180°C, 350°F, Gas Mark 4. Grease a 20 cm (8 inch) square cake tin.

Sift the flour with the salt into a mixing bowl. Make a well in the centre and pour in the cooled chocolate mixture. Using a wooden spoon, gradually draw the flour into the liquid, then beat in the eggs and walnuts. Stir well to mix, adding enough milk to make a soft dropping consistency.

Pour the mixture into the prepared tin. Bake in the oven for about 30 minutes, or until a skewer inserted in the centre comes out clean. Leave to cool completely in tin. Cut into squares.

Serving ideas: Serve the brownies by themselves for tea or with vanilla ice cream as a dessert.

Peanut cookies

MAKES ABOUT 18

50 g (2 oz) smooth peanut butter
50 g (2 oz) margarine or butter,
   softened
2 tsp grated orange rind
50 g (2 oz) caster sugar
40 g (1 ½ oz) soft light brown sugar
pinch of ground allspice
½ egg, beaten
40 g (1 ½ oz) sultanas, chopped
100 g (4 oz) self-raising flour
25-40 g (1-1 ½ oz) unsalted peanuts,
   chopped

Heat the oven to 180°C, 350°F, Gas Mark 4. Cream the peanut butter with the margarine in a bowl until light and fluffy. Add the orange rind and sugars and allspice, if using, and beat again. Beat in the egg, then the sultanas and flour. Mix to a firm dough.

Roll into balls about the size of a walnut and place fairly well apart on lightly greased baking sheets. Flatten each biscuit slightly and mark a criss-cross pattern on top with a fork. Sprinkle with chopped peanuts.

Bake in the oven for about 25 minutes, or until golden brown. Transfer to a wire rack and cool completely.

Variation: Replace the peanuts with hazelnuts and peanut butter with hazelnut spread.

Chocolate fruit bars

MAKES 12

90g (3½oz) butter
1 tbls golden syrup
225g (8oz) muesli
25g (1oz) seedless raisins, chopped
50g (2oz) glacé cherries, finely
  chopped
25g (1oz) angelica, chopped
100g (4oz) plain chocolate
12 glacé cherry halves, to decorate

Grease an 18cm (7 inch) square shallow tin.

Melt the butter in a small saucepan over gentle heat and stir in the syrup. Remove from the heat and stir in the muesli, raisins, cherries and angelica.

Press the mixture into the prepared tin.

Place the chocolate in a heatproof bowl set over a saucepan of hot water and heat gently, stirring, until melted. Spread the melted chocolate over the mixture in the tin and mark decoratively with a fork. Decorate with the cherry halves. Chill in the refrigerator until firm, then cut into bars.

Serving idea: These make ideal teatime treats.
Variation: Replace the melted chocolate with chocolate-flavoured cake covering.

● Left: Chocolate fruit bars;
Right: Peanut cookies

Cucumber and sausage caterpillar

SERVES 12

1 large cucumber, preferably slightly
 curved
2 glacé cherries
450 g (1 lb) cocktail sausages
6 streaky bacon rashers, rinded and
 halved crossways
227 g (8 oz) can pineapple pieces,
 drained
198 g (7 oz) can mandarins
125 G (4 oz) mild cheese, cubed

Cutting at a slant, slice off the thicker end of the cucumber. To make the eyes, spear each cherry on to the end of a halved cocktail stick and press the sticks in either side of the cut end of the cucumber.

Using a sharp knife, make a few small cuts about 3 mm (⅛ inch) apart, across the cucumber at the other end for the tail. Heat the grill to moderate.

Prick the sausages with a fork, place in a frying pan and fry gently for about 8 minutes, turning to brown on all sides.

Meanwhile, wrap each half bacon rasher around a piece of pineapple and secure with a wooden cocktail stick. Grill the bacon and pineapple rolls for 3-4 minutes until the bacon is crisp. Drain on absorbent kitchen paper.

Drain the fried sausages on absorbent kitchen paper and spear each one with a cocktail stick. Stick the sausages in a row down the centre of the cucumber. Stick the bacon and pineapple rolls on either side with the mandarins on top of cubed cheese in between. Serve at once.

Variations: If you can't find cocktail sausages, buy chipolatas and twist each sausage in the middle, then cut in half.

Pizza face fingers

SERVES 10-12

300 g (12 oz) self-raising flour
2 tsp salt
75 g (3 oz) margarine, diced
1 egg
150 ml (¼ pint) milk
For the topping
1 tbls vegetable oil
2 large onions, roughly chopped
1 small green pepper, cored, seeded
 and roughly chopped
397 g (14 oz) can tomatoes
2 tbls tomato purée
1 small bay leaf
½ tsp paprika
salt and pepper
To decorate
handful cooked peas
about 50 g (2 oz) mushrooms, sliced
4-6 slices salami
75 g (3 oz) Cheddar cheese, grated
1 tbls vegetable oil

To make the topping, heat the oil in a saucepan, add the onions and cook gently for 5 minutes until softened. Add the green pepper, tomatoes with their juice, tomato purée, bay leaf and paprika and season to taste.

Bring to the boil, then reduce the heat, cover and simmer for 15 minutes. Uncover and cook for a further 10 minutes until reduced by half.

Remove from the heat and allow to cool slightly. Discard the bay leaf. Place the tomato mixture in a blender goblet and process until puréed, or pass through a sieve. Adjust the seasoning to taste. Set aside to cool.

To make the pizza dough, sift the flour with the salt into a bowl. Add the margarine and rub in with the fingertips until the mixture resembles fine breadcrumbs. Beat the egg with the milk. Gradually mix into the dry ingredients to make a soft dough. Turn the dough on to a floured surface and knead lightly until smooth.

Heat the oven to 200°C, 400°F, Gas Mark 6. Grease a shallow 33 × 23 cm (13 × 9 inch) baking tin. Roll out the dough to a 35 × 25 cm (14 × 10 inch) rectangle and use to line the tin, pushing it well into the sides and corners. Spread the tomato topping over the dough.

Prepare the 'face' decoration. Use one pea for each eye and a mushroom slice for the nose. Cut a salami crescent shape for each mouth. Arrange as 'faces' in 2 or 3 rows on top of the pizza, using the grated cheese for hair. Drizzle over the oil.

Bake in the oven for about 35 minutes or until the dough is risen and golden brown. Serve hot or warm, cut into wedges with a face on each one.

Serving idea: Garnish the pizza with plenty of watercress sprigs and tomato wedges.

Variations: Sliced mushroom stalks could be used for eyes and sliced mushroom caps for mouths. Pieces of red or green pepper could also be used for the mouths.

● Pizza face fingers; Cucumber and sausage caterpillar

Cheesy sausage rolls

MAKES ABOUT 24

225 g (8 oz) plain flour
½ tsp salt
pinch of English mustard powder
pinch of cayenne pepper
75 g (3 oz) margarine, diced
50 g (2 oz) Cheddar cheese, grated
2 tbls cold water
225 g (8 oz) sausagemeat
milk, to glaze

Sift the flour with the salt, mustard and cayenne into a bowl. Add the margarine and rub in with the fingertips until the mixture resembles fine breadcrumbs. Stir in the cheese. Add the water and mix to a firm dough. Heat the oven to 200°C, 400°F, Gas Mark 6.

Turn the dough on to a lightly floured work surface and knead lightly. Roll out fairly thinly to form a rectangle. Trim the edges and cut lengthways into two strips.

Divide the sausagemeat into 2 equal portions and dust each with flour. Shape into two rolls the length of the dough. Lay a sausagemeat roll down the centre of one piece of dough. Brush the long dough edges with milk and press firmly together to seal. Repeat with the remaining dough and sausagemeat.

Brush the sausagemeat rolls all over with milk. Cut crossways into 2.5-4 cm (1-1½ inch) pieces and arrange on a large baking sheet.

Bake in the oven for 15 minutes, then reduce the oven temperature to 180°C, 350°F, Gas Mark 4 and bake for a further 15 minutes, or until golden.

Serving ideas: Sausage rolls are favourite party fare, whether they are served hot, warm or cold. They are also popular for picnics and packed lunches, or as a snack.
Variations: Omit the mustard powder and cayenne from the dough ingredients. Spread the sausagemeat with a little tomato ketchup or sweet pickle before covering with the pastry.

Peanut balls

MAKES ABOUT 24

225 g (8 oz) full fat soft cheese
2 tbls crunchy peanut butter
75 g (3 oz) ham, finely chopped
3 tbls fresh wholemeal breadcrumbs
100 g (4 oz) salted or dry roast
  peanuts, finely chopped

Using a wooden spoon, beat the cheese with the peanut butter in a bowl until light and fluffy. Stir in the chopped ham and the breadcrumbs and beat until thoroughly combined.

Divide the mixture into about 24 portions and shape into balls. Roll in chopped peanuts to coat evenly.

Serving ideas: For older children, spear the peanut balls on coloured cocktail sticks; for younger children, simply arrange the savouries in a serving dish.

56

Animal cheese biscuits

MAKES 50

225 g (8 oz) plain flour
pinch of salt
¼ tsp English mustard powder
100 g (4 oz) margarine or butter, diced
75 g (3 oz) strong Cheddar cheese,
*   finely grated*
1 egg yolk
2 tbls water
a little milk, for glazing
sesame seeds, to finish

Heat the oven to 200°C, 400°F, Gas Mark 6.

Sift the flour with the salt and mustard powder into a mixing bowl. Add the margarine and rub it in with the fingertips until the mixture resembles fine breadcrumbs. Add the egg yolk and water and mix in with a knife, then draw the dough together with your hands and shape into a ball.

Turn the dough on to a lightly floured work surface and knead lightly until smooth. Wrap in foil or cling film and chill in the refrigerator for 30 minutes.

Roll out the dough on a lightly floured work surface to a 2 mm (⅛ inch) thickness. Using a different-shaped animal cutter, cut out shapes and place them fairly well apart on 2 large greased baking sheets. Brush all over with milk and use a skewer to make holes for eyes, noses and mouths. Sprinkle the biscuits with sesame seeds.

Bake in the oven for 15-20 minutes, switching the baking sheets halfway through baking time, until golden brown. Remove from the oven, leave to cool for 1-2 minutes, then carefully transfer to a wire rack and cool completely.

● Cheesy sausage rolls; Peanut balls; Animal cheese biscuits

Engine cake

100 g (4 oz) icing sugar
50 g (2 oz) margarine
2 tbls drinking chocolate
4 strips liquorice
8 mini chocolate-covered Swiss rolls
1 large chocolate-covered Swiss roll
1 chocolate sponge sandwich cake
4 iced fondant cakes
* To finish
50 g (2 oz) smarties
15 g (½ oz) chocolate vermicelli
50 g (2 oz) dolly mixtures
1 liquorice Catherine wheel
1 chocolate-covered marshmallow
   biscuit
½ mini chocolate-covered Swiss roll
¼ large chocolate-covered Swiss roll

Make chocolate butter icing by beating the icing sugar and margarine together, then stirring in the drinking chocolate. Spread half the icing over a cake board. Arrange 2 strips of liquorice down the centre of the board to resemble train rails, and put 4 of the chocolate mini rolls across the rails, to make wheels. Arrange the large Swiss roll on top of the mini rolls to represent the engine.

Put a further 2 mini rolls across the rails. Cut a square from the chocolate sandwich cake, to represent the tender, and spread with a little chocolate butter icing (underneath side). Arrange on top of the mini rolls behind the engine. Put the remaining 2 mini rolls behind the engine tender. Cut one rectangle about the length of a mini roll from the remainder of the sponge sandwich, open out, and place the two halves across the two mini rolls. Top with the iced fondant cakes.

Decorate the cake board with smarties. Spread a little butter icing on top of the tender, cover with chocolate vermicelli and pile some of the dolly

mixtures on top.

Stick the liquorice Catherine wheel on to the front edge of the engine and put the marshmallow biscuit on top of the engine at the front edge. Place half a mini chocolate covered roll behind it to make a chimney and top with the remaining dolly mixtures. Finally, make the cab by fixing the ¼ piece of large chocolate Swiss roll behind the chimney. Pipe the remaining chocolate cream icing decoratively around the biscuit, chimney and cab before serving.

Serving idea: This cake is ideal for a boy's birthday.
Variation: Use liquorice allsorts as well as the dolly mixture to decorate.

● **Butterfly birthday cake;**
Right: Engine cake

Butterfly birthday cake

2 × 20 cm (8 inch) round chocolate
Victoria sandwich cakes
For the buttercream
225 g (8 oz) unsalted butter
450 g (1 lb) icing sugar, sifted
a few drops of vanilla essence
1-2 tbls milk
pink food colouring
For the apricot glaze
225 g (8 oz) apricot jam
2 tbls water
To decorate
assorted small sweets
2 strips of angelica (optional)

To make the buttercream, cream the butter in a bowl until light and fluffy and gradually beat in the icing sugar. Beat in the vanilla essence and milk.

Use a little of the buttercream to sandwich the cakes together.

To make the apricot glaze, heat the jam and water in a heavy-based saucepan until the jam is melted, then sieve. Return to the pan and bring to the boil. Simmer gently until the mixture will coat the back of a wooden spoon. Remove from the heat and set aside to cool.

Cut the cake in half crossways. Position the halves back-to-back on a cake board at a slightly slanting angle so that the 'wings' are wider apart at the top. Brush the cakes all over with apricot glaze.

Coat the top and sides of the cake with two-thirds of the buttercream.

Tint the remaining buttercream pink. Place in a piping bag fitted with a fine star nozzle and pipe rosettes around the edge of each wing.

Decorate the wings with bright patterns of coloured sweets, such as dolly mixtures, smarties, or coloured balls. Put a line of sweets down the middle to represent the 'body' of the butterfly.

Pipe a border of the pink buttercream all round the base of the butterfly. Leave to set.

Complete the cake with two long strips of angelica for antennae, if wished.

Home-made fudge

MAKES 450 g (1 lb)

175 ml (6 fl oz) condensed milk
50 g (2 oz) unsalted butter, diced
175 g (6 oz) soft light brown sugar
50 g (2 oz) granulated sugar
100 g (4 oz) powdered glucose
120 ml (4 fl oz) water
a few drops of vanilla essence

Line the base of an 18 cm (7 inch) square shallow tin with oiled grease-proof or non-stick silicone paper.

Place the condensed milk and butter in a heatproof bowl set over a pan of hot water and heat gently until melted. Remove from the heat and set aside.

Place the sugars, glucose and water in a saucepan and heat gently, stirring frequently, until dissolved. Continue to boil, without stirring until the soft ball stage is reached, 115°C (238°F). To test for this, drop a teaspoon of the syrup into iced water. Mould the sticky syrup into a soft ball with the fingers. Remove the ball from the water. It should immediately lose its shape.

Remove the pan from the heat and, using a wooden spoon, stir the condensed milk mixture into the sugar syrup. Return the pan to the heat and heat gently then bring to the boil, stirring continuously, until the mixture regains the soft ball temperature.

Dip the base of the pan briefly into cold water to stop it heating further, then beat for 5 minutes. Pour evenly into the prepared tin and leave to set.

When almost firm, mark into squares, using an oiled knife. Leave until quite firm, then cut into squares and store for up to 4 weeks in an airtight tin.

Variation: For chocolate fudge, melt 100 g (4 oz) plain chocolate with the condensed milk and butter.

Party volcano cake

SERVES 12

1 litre (2 pints) or 2 family blocks
    chocolate and orange ice cream
600 ml (1 pint) or 1 family block
    vanilla ice cream
75 g (3 oz) chocolate polka dots
4 tsp grated orange rind
85 ml (3 fl oz) raspberry syrup

Remove the ice creams from the freezer and allow to soften in the refrigerator for 45 minutes.

Using a large round serving plate or cake board about 25 cm (10 inches) in diameter, scoop or spoon the chocolate ice cream on to it to form a mound. Top this with the vanilla ice cream to represent a snow-capped mountain. Work as quickly as you can so that the effect of the cake is not lost as the ice cream melts.

Make a small well in the top of the 'mountain' to form a crater. Sprinkle chocolate dots over the lower half of the cake to represent rolling boulders and scatter grated orange rind over the upper half to represent falling sparks.

Pour the raspberry syrup into the 'crater' and allow it to trickle down the 'mountain'. Serve immediately.

Serving idea: For a really special effect, top the volcano cake with a lit sparkler placed firmly in a birthday cake candle holder as it is brought to the table. This finishing touch would only be suitable for younger children under adult supervision.

Variation: Any partly-chocolate flavoured ice cream could be used. Choc-mint ice cream would be a good choice.

• Party volcano cake; Home-made fudge

Peach, apple and ginger fizz

SERVES 4

2 medium peaches, peeled, stoned and chopped
120 ml (4 fl oz) apple juice, chilled
600 ml (1 pint) ginger ale, chilled
crushed ice
apple slices, to decorate, optional

Place the peaches and apple juice in a blender goblet and process until smooth. With the machine still running, add the ginger ale.

Place crushed ice in each of 4 tumblers and pour over the fizzy drink. Decorate with an apple slice if using, and serve immediately while still frothy.

Variations: Use orange juice instead of apple juice. Replace the ginger ale with lemonade.

● Left: Peach, apple and ginger fizz; Centre: Caribbean cocktail; Right: Strawberry milk shake

Strawberry milk shake

SERVES 2

300 ml (½ pint) milk, chilled
100 g (4 oz) strawberries, hulled if
fresh, thawed if frozen
1 tbls caster sugar

Place the milk, strawberries and sugar in a blender goblet and process for 10-15 seconds.
 Strain into 2 chilled glasses and serve immediately.

Serving idea: Top each milk shake with a scoop of strawberry ice cream. Provide straws to drink with.
Variations: Use 4 tbls drained canned strawberries instead of fresh or frozen ones. Use fresh, frozen or canned raspberries instead of strawberries, or use 4 tbls crushed pineapple or 3 pineapple rings, chopped.

Caribbean cocktail

SERVES 4

1 cm (½ inch) thick slice of fresh
pineapple, peeled, or 1 pineapple
ring, drained
2 ripe bananas
9 tbls fresh orange juice
8 ice cubes
1 tsp lime juice
crushed ice
2 pineapple rings, halved, to decorate,
optional

Place the pineapple, bananas, orange juice, ice cubes and lime juice in a blender goblet and process until smooth.
 Place crushed ice in each of 4 tall chilled glasses and pour in the cocktail. Decorate the rim of each glass with a piece of pineapple if using.

INDEX